"Frank Early has written an instructional book that all levels of the game can benefit from and enjoy."
—Butch Buchholz
Chairman and founder of the Lipton Championships

"Frank Early's book is innovative and informative; following his advice will have an immediate, positive impact on your game."
—Cliff Drysdale
ESPN analyst and former U.S. Open Doubles champion

"Frank's teaching is provocative, unique, and effective."
—Vitas Gerulaitis
Former CBS analyst and Australian Open Singles champion

"*Tennis Strokes That Win* offers clear, solid instruction."
—Roy Emerson
Winner of 28 Grand Slam tournaments

TENNIS
STROKES THAT
WIN

Breakthrough Techniques
for Mastering the Game

FRANK EARLY
PHOTOGRAPHS BY RON BERNSTEIN

CONTEMPORARY
BOOKS
A TRIBUNE NEW MEDIA COMPANY

Library of Congress Cataloging-in-Publication Data

Early, Frank, 1962–
   Tennis strokes that win : breakthrough techniques for
mastering the game / Frank Early.
        p.   cm.
    Includes index.

    1. Tennis.   I. Title.
GV995.E27   1995
796.342'2—dc20   95-17293
                                                        CIP

Cover photo by Eugen Gebhardt/FPG
Interior photos by Ron Bernstein
Back-cover photo © Eva Lipton

Published by Contemporary Books, Inc.
Two Prudential Plaza, Chicago, Illinois 60601-6790
Manufactured in the United States of America
International Standard Book Number: 0-8092-3447-5
10   9   8   7   6   5   4   3   2   1

To my father, Frank H. Early,
and to my nephew, Bryan S. Early

Contents

Acknowledgments

For assistance during preparation of the manuscript, my thanks to Steve Foldes, Charlie McGowen, Joseph Peel, and Peter Schmitt.

Thanks to Eva, Lauren, and Talia for their love and support.

Special thanks to Ron Bernstein, a great photographer and an even greater friend.

Introduction

This book was designed to help you do one thing: improve your strokes. Of course, there is more to tennis than hitting the ball. To play your best, you may need to make improvements in other areas, such as strategy, mental toughness, or physical fitness. Improving your strokes can help you make improvements in all of these areas.

You can't execute a strategy if you can't control the ball: improving your strokes makes even the simplest strategy more effective. You can't be mentally tough if you don't have confidence in your shot-making ability: improving your strokes builds confidence and mental toughness. You can't improve your physical fitness if you spend more time picking up balls than hitting them: improving your strokes simultaneously improves your physical fitness.

Just as a basketball player must be able to control the ball, and a hockey player must be able to control the puck, most of a tennis player's success depends on his or her ability to control the tennis ball. Ultimately, your strokes are the tools that get the job done.

This book does not advocate a particular style. Numerous styles can be applied to every stroke. Observe ten players who have exceptional forehands, and you will probably see ten different styles: eastern grips and western grips, open stances and closed stances, straight backswings and looped backswings. Compare the two photographs of Goran Ivanisevic on pages xiv and xv: Both shots are backhand groundstrokes, but note the difference in the position of Ivanisevic's feet. Now focus on how these two shots are similar. The strokes of a highly skilled player may look different from one shot to the next, but the most essential qualities of the stroke will remain constant. This book does not stress the differences between good strokes; it stresses what good strokes have in common.

Players of all abilities who are ready to begin the improvement process can benefit from seeking out the common qualities of good strokes. While there is an obvious disparity between the skills of a world-class player and those of a recreational player, both are capable of achieving a high degree of positive change in the quality of their tennis. The world-class player is more likely to win Wimbledon, but he or she is not more or less likely to improve. As a teaching pro for the past twelve years, I have never seen a lack of athletic skills get in the way of anyone with a sincere desire to play better tennis.

Significant improvement does not come immediately; it is a process that requires patience and tolerance. Some players are easily frustrated by the process and abandon any hope for improvement; others are satisfied with marginal improvement but never experience a substantial change.

I have been fortunate to work with hundreds of players who have experienced a continuous process of substantial improvement. After reflecting on these players as a group, it has become clear to me that there is no connection between a player's age or athletic ability and the degree of improvement that he or she is capable of achieving. Despite some obvious differences, these players share common qualities that facilitate the improvement process: they are willing to experiment, they invest the time and energy necessary to reinforce the things that work, and they love playing the game. Without exception, these three qualities must be present for a substantial improvement to occur.

To improve your tennis, you must be willing to experiment. Improvement requires problem-solving skills, and there is usually more than one effective solution to any problem. Experimentation is the only way to explore the possibilities. Bjorn Borg's solutions were different from John McEnroe's; Martina Navratilova's solutions were different from Chris Evert's. Great minds don't think alike, and the same instruction does not always produce the same results. If a particular piece of advice makes sense to you, give it your best shot; if it doesn't work, you can try something else.

Improving your tennis takes a sincere and dynamic commitment. Experiment until you find the most encouraging results; then give it your time, your patience, your sweat, and make it work. Without this commitment, no amount of instruction will help you improve. Make the commitment and anything is possible.

To improve your tennis, you've got to love playing the game. This needs no explanation.

Remember that this book can be instructive as long as you are willing to put the information to the test. Give it your best shot, and remember to have fun with it.

Goran Ivanisevic closes the stance on this two-handed stroke. Compare this photograph with the one on the right: the position of the body is similar from the waist up but radically different from the waist down. The differences in good strokes may be more dramatic than the similarities, but observing those similarities is the key to discovering the essential qualities of good strokes.

For this shot, Ivanisevic uses an open stance. Neither stance is incorrect for a two-handed stroke. The exact position of his feet from one shot to the next will be dictated by his sense of balance and timing. What do these strokes have in common? In both examples, Ivanisevic maintains head stability and uses a balanced hip and shoulder rotation to provide the force of his swing.

TENNIS
STROKES THAT
WIN

The Meaning of Stroke Efficiency

Efficiency means achieving effective results with little waste of effort. In order to hit consistently effective shots over an extended period of time, you must achieve a high degree of stroke efficiency. Although you may not have been aware of it at the time, you began to pursue efficiency when you decided that you wanted to improve your tennis.

Efficiency is the best way to ensure longevity. It is no coincidence that Ken Rosewall has had the most successful long-term playing career in the history of tennis while employing some of the most efficient strokes ever to grace a court. Whether we consider a single match, a tournament, or an entire career, those players who develop efficient strokes are the ones most likely to maintain effectiveness for the duration.

An efficient stroke provides the most effective shot that a given amount of effort can produce. Imagine two players evenly matched in speed, strength, strategy, and mental toughness; they are equally determined to win and use equal amounts of effort to execute their strokes. If the strokes of one of these players are more efficient, then his or her shots will be more effective.

Strokes that don't produce effective shots—regardless of how smooth and graceful they may appear—cannot be described as efficient. One particular double fault may require less effort than another, but if winning points is the desired effect, there is no such thing as an efficient double fault.

While an efficient stroke may seem effortless when compared to an inefficient stroke, efficiency should not be confused with effortlessness. Since *effortless* means "done without effort," only spectators can achieve true effortlessness.

The overall effort used to execute a stroke can originate from various power sources. Depending on the type of stroke, some power sources are better than others. The two most significant sources of power for the production of efficient strokes are *hip and shoulder rotation* and *weight transfer*. With these as your primary power sources, you will create a foundation for efficient strokes from every position on the court.

THE EFFICIENCY OF HIP AND SHOULDER ROTATION

Every tennis stroke imaginable requires rotation of various parts of the body. In mechanical terms, rotational movement is not just the most natural type of movement we can execute—it is the *only* type of movement we can execute. Even actions that *appear* to move in a straight line are actually the end results of a complex series of rotations of various parts of the body.

Rotation of the hips and shoulders is of special significance in swinging a tennis racket. The hips and shoulders are effective reference points because they are, quite literally, the central gears of the swing system. In *The Mechanics of Athletics* (New York: Holmes & Meier, 1962), Geoffrey Dyson examines the mechanics of shot-putting to show how a natural sequence of movement begins around the body's center of gravity and progresses outward. He makes it clear that the principle also applies to most other athletic events:

> Contrary to the view that the putting action "is a movement which begins in the toes and ends in the fingers," in fact *(as in almost all athletic activities) movement begins in the stronger but slower muscles surrounding the athlete's center of gravity and is then taken up, below the hips, at the knees, ankles and feet, in that order; simultaneously, above the hips, it extends upwards through the putting shoulder, elbow, wrist, and fingers.* . . . Therefore, a technically sound putting action can be likened to the throwing of a stone into a pool of water—causing the ripples to flow outward.

An efficient swing is a series of rotational movements that flow in an instantaneous sequence: your hips and shoulders are the largest and most powerful gears to be engaged in that sequence. Developing an efficient hip and shoulder rotation reinforces balance because it will encourage you to use the center of your body as an axis; leverage is reinforced because contact with the ground is necessary to initiate rotation. As a result of the elastic action of muscles between the hips and shoulders (elasticity will be discussed in more detail in Chapter 3), a relatively small degree of hip and shoulder rotation can account for a high proportion of the swing's over-all force.

Stepping into the ball and transferring weight in the direction of your shot can contribute to the effectiveness of a swinging stroke. In fact, many actions other than hip and shoulder rotation can contribute to an effective swing, but when a properly timed and balanced rotation is not a source of power for your swing, other actions are merely compensations.

THE EFFICIENCY OF WEIGHT TRANSFER

While hip and shoulder rotation is a natural and effective way to generate force, it is not an efficient source of power for all strokes.

The low volley is an example of a stroke in which hip and shoulder rotation can be detrimental. In most low-volley situations, the amount of racket-head speed generated by hip and shoulder rotation isn't necessary. Additionally, the low volley is a relatively quick-reflex stroke, and time limitations make the use of a complete rotation impractical. Furthermore, the sudden lunging and reaching required for many low volleys can inhibit the leverage for an effective rotation to occur. The low volley is an example of a stroke in which one should place an emphasis on weight transfer instead of hip and shoulder rotation.

Using weight transfer will encourage you to move your feet, and good footwork is critical in quick-reflex situations. Watch great volleyers and you will see that foot movement does not simply get them into position for the stroke: *foot movement is a part of the stroke.* Using weight transfer will also encourage you to move forward. Moving forward allows you to intercept the shot sooner, which decreases your opponent's reaction time and increases the amount of possible angles for your shot. Furthermore, learning to use weight transfer will allow you to make effective shots while you are in the process of approaching the net or lunging for an oncoming ball.

Two Efficient Power Sources, Three Types of Strokes

Any stroke can be placed into one of three categories based on the stroke's most significant source of power. Hip and shoulder rotation is the most significant source of power for *swinging strokes*, such as groundstrokes and serves. Weight transfer is the most significant source of power for *punching strokes*, such as volleys and half-volleys. Usually, these power sources do not function independently: some weight transfer is present during a swing, and a small amount of trunk rotation is present during a punch. While some strokes require a predominant power source, other strokes require a more balanced combination of both sources. Approach shots and high volleys are examples of *combined strokes*.

Before exploring specifics of these three types of strokes, it is important to review some of the principles that apply to all strokes; these fundamental reminders are presented in Chapter 2. Swinging strokes, punching strokes, and combined strokes are covered in Chapters 3, 4, and 5, respectively.

Rotate back: *Jennifer Capriati has coiled her hips and shoulders and is about to unload on a backhand. Note that her hands and racket head stay in front of the plane of her shoulders: at this phase of the swing, she is initiating a stretch of the trunk muscles, not the arm muscles.*

Rotate forward: *Monica Seles demonstrates a powerful forward rotation on the two-handed forehand. Her upper body stays relatively vertical and her stance is open. Most of the natural weight transfer that occurs during this swing moves from left to right, not back to front. For powerful and efficient swinging strokes, a balanced hip and shoulder rotation is more significant than a pronounced transfer of weight.*

Step on it: *Richard Krajicek uses weight transfer as a power source for the forehand volley. He is in the process of stepping forward as he makes contact. If he had completed his step before contact, he would have exhausted most of the force provided by weight transfer.*

Step on it: *Instead of simply reaching for this volley, Jana Novotna drives her weight forward. Notice that her front foot is still off the court an instant before her racket makes contact with the ball.*

Fundamental Reminders

A competitive match can be a form of practice. It is possible to compete while "working out" certain aspects of your game. In fact, there are some lessons that can be learned only through competition: anyone who has ever scraped to save a break point knows that the urgency of the situation cannot be simulated. A competitive match, however, is not the time to work on your strokes.

Suppose you have a black belt in karate and you are attacked in an alley by a gang of thugs. Will you worry about correct form, or will you simply kick their lights out? When time is limited, thinking is a big mistake. Likewise, a match is not the time to think about or experiment with your strokes, and this is why practice is so important. Practice is the time to experiment, but mostly, it is time to rehearse your strokes so they become familiar and dependable.

In any discussion of tennis strokes, it is important to distinguish a rehearsed stroke from an improvised stroke. A rehearsed stroke is acquired through practicing at a controllable pace with the simple objective of hitting reliable, effective shots. An improvised stroke is a spontaneous reaction that occurs during match play or fast-paced drills when the objective is doing whatever it takes to win.

An improvised stroke is usually inefficient, but it may be the only way to save a point. While relying entirely on improvised strokes is an impractical approach to winning, one rarely wins a close match on rehearsed strokes alone. Work to avoid match situations where an improvised stroke is the only option, but accept that those situations are bound to occur. When you see no other option, don't hesitate to improvise unless the attempt runs the risk of injury. Resorting to an improvised stroke does not insult your talent; it complements your will to win.

In order to develop and maintain efficient stroke production, you must create a routine of rehearsing your strokes in a noncompetitive atmosphere. Of the thousands of excuses for not practicing, the most absurd is that too much stroke rehearsal will make you an unimaginative, human-ball-machine type of player. In all of my years of coaching, I have never heard a player say, "I'm tired of hitting one terrific shot after another."

▶

Improvise: *Given a choice, Aranxta Sanchez-Vicario would prefer to hit a shot with more offensive possibilities. At this moment, she is not interested in developing her stroke production; she will run and stretch for as many shots as it takes to win this point. During a match, expect to hit many strokes that you do not rehearse in a noncompetitive practice session.*

The least imaginative thing you can do is to continually rely on your ability to improvise. Improvisation is necessary when the situation controls you; imagination is necessary to control the situation. Rehearsing your strokes will never make you unimaginative. To the contrary, the more situations you rehearse, the more imaginative your range of options. Rehearse your strokes in a wide variety of situations, and it will be your opponent who will have to resort to improvised strokes.

SET SHORT-TERM GOALS

As students of tennis, we share some common long-term goals. Whether recreational player or Wimbledon champion, we all want to hit the right shot at the right time, experience our full potential, and enjoy the process. In addition to these common goals, we have individual goals, such as hitting a more consistent backhand, adding pace to our serve, or becoming more aggressive at net.

Achieving long-term goals is one of the most satisfying rewards of the sport. When it comes to strokes, the most reliable way to reach a long-term goal is through a series of systematic, short-term goals. For example, suppose that your long-term goal is to hit a more powerful forehand. While rehearsing your stroke, you discover that you are hitting the ball too late. Now you have an immediate short-term goal: hit the ball earlier. As you try to hit the ball earlier, you find that your stroke becomes rushed and uncontrollable. In order to regain control, you may have to rotate your upper body sooner during the preparation sequence. Now you have a second short-term goal: rotate sooner. The logical, systematic approach to these short-term goals is to rehearse an earlier rotation first, then rehearse hitting the ball farther in front. The former will make it easier to achieve the latter.

Early rotation and hitting farther in front may bring you closer to your long-term goal, but it may not be enough. Achieving more consistent power may require modifications of other aspects of the stroke, such as balance, footwork, and racket-head velocity. Given the limited time available to execute the stroke, however, it would be counterproductive to try to achieve all of your short-term goals at once. Concentrate on one or two short-term goals, and use simple reminders, or cues, to help reinforce the necessary modifications. With the short-term goals mentioned above, your cues could be "turn," and "hit in front." Once you feel that the modifications have become instinctive, reexamine the stroke to find what additional modifications are necessary and create a new set of cues.

Improvement is not always a simple, linear process. It is not unusual that a small adjustment of one particular part of a stroke will have an initial, negative impact on other parts of the stroke. Hang in there: that small adjustment might lead to a substantial increase in overall efficiency. Much of your improvement will depend on your ability to tolerate the breakdowns before experiencing the breakthroughs.

It may take a few days or even a few weeks to define your short-term goals, and it may take considerably longer to achieve those goals and then to assemble them in a smooth, reliable sequence. Be patient as you explore your goals. Change is growth, and growth takes time. Remember, if tennis were easy, it wouldn't be any fun.

LET IT FLOW

If we had to concentrate on each of the various manipulations required to tie our shoes, most of us would wear sandals. From a mechanical standpoint, tying our shoes is complicated. Unless you have young children, you may have forgotten the process of learning the task: make a loop with one end of the lace, wrap the other end around that loop, and so on. It wasn't easy at first, but we set some short-term goals, rehearsed the movements, and eventually we all became experts.

John Wooden, UCLA's legendary basketball coach, would say to freshmen on their first day of practice: "Today, you are going to learn to tie your shoes." This was a lesson on paying attention to detail, a lesson on viewing habitual movements in a new light, and a subtle reminder that practice can turn a complex series of actions into a simple routine.

As you work to refine the various aspects of your strokes, it is important to remember that a tennis stroke is not a collection of disconnected actions. The action of a specific body part must always be considered in the context of how it enhances or inhibits the overall effort of the stroke. *An efficient stroke is a series of actions that flow in an instantaneous sequence.* Ultimately, hitting a tennis ball should feel as natural as tying your shoes.

Your muscles must be appropriately relaxed in order for the separate actions of the stroke to flow. How can you be relaxed while you are running around on a tennis court? The same way you are relaxed when you are dancing. When you dance to an up-tempo song, your body is moving rapidly, but your muscles are loose and relaxed; you are letting the movements flow. Ultimately, hitting a tennis ball should feel as relaxed as dancing.

MAINTAIN BALANCE

In order for your muscles to achieve an appropriate degree of relaxation, you must maintain balance as you execute your strokes. Unbalanced strokes create inefficiency and fatigue, and—as if that's not enough—they look bad. Aesthetics aside, the way a stroke looks can reveal a weakness: if opponents recognize that one of your strokes is consistently off balance, they will know which one is most likely to break down. The causes of poor balance can be traced to three specific areas: The lower body (see page 18), head stability (see page 22), and the position of the contact point (see page 27).

It is possible to compensate for certain inadequacies of stroke production. For example, timing may compensate for a lack of speed, or stamina may compensate for a lack of strength. Nothing, however, can compensate for a lack of balance.

Whether swinging or punching, the force of an efficient stroke travels from your center of gravity to the racket head in an instantaneous sequence. A loss of balance at the *beginning* of a stroke will inhibit your body's ability to initiate force. A loss of balance *during* a stroke will inhibit your body's ability to transfer force to the racket.

Balance is a universal reference point for all strokes. Should you use an open or closed stance on wide forehands? How much backswing should you use on a backhand approach shot? How far in front of your body should you toss the ball when serving? Experiment as you rehearse your strokes, and when you find the most-balanced options, you will have found the answers.

In most situations, excessive waist flexion will lead to an off-balance stroke. However, when a stroke is executed as your body rapidly accelerates to the ball, waist flexion is an essential part of maintaining balance. Imagine a sprinter as he leaves the starting block: his upper body will tilt forward. The sprinter's posture will become straighter after several steps, but in order to maintain balance during his initial burst of acceleration, he must flex at the waist and lean into the direction of his movement. Likewise, whenever you are rapidly accelerating to an approaching ball, waist flexion is necessary for maintaining balance. An off-balance stroke will occur when you flex at the waist without flexing the knees as well.

In situations where you are not rapidly accelerating to an oncoming shot, excessive waist flexion will always be detrimental. As long as momentum is not forcing you to flex at the waist, stay relatively vertical from the waist up. If your head or shoulders tilt forward, backward, or sideways as you execute your stroke, you are either consciously attempting to hit the ball beyond the effective contact range, or your legs have failed you. In both cases, balance is diminished.

Keeping your head, shoulders, and hips in a vertical line will help ensure that you are getting down for low balls by flexing your knees; it will also help ensure that you are moving your feet for wide balls instead of simply reaching for them. Furthermore, it will reinforce head stability and a consistent contact range. All of these qualities contribute to better balance.

MOVE YOUR FEET AND BEND YOUR KNEES

The movement of your lower body is the foundation for balance and efficiency. Your feet, in contact with the court, provide leverage for all strokes. Your knees, flexing and extending, make it possible for force to transfer through the body in a smooth and efficient sequence.

Because your lower body does the additional and often exhausting task of moving you from one shot to the next, it is easy to experience a "leg lapse" during the execution of your stroke. A leg lapse means that your body has an inefficient base of support due to poor footwork or knee flexion.

▶

Maintain balance: *Even when being stretched to the limit, the left half of Ivan Lendl's body balances the right half of his body. See pages 59–61 for more examples of good balance on the one-handed backhand.*

A leg lapse causes the upper body to compensate for the loss of leverage, resulting in a stroke that is off balance, inefficient, and usually ineffective.

The most common example of a leg lapse occurs when a shot is wide to either side of your body and you simply reach for it instead of moving your feet. The second most common leg lapse occurs when a shot is low and you flex at the waist without flexing the knees.

Fatigue is the number one cause of leg lapses; general laziness takes a close second. The best way to avoid fatigue and laziness is by conditioning your lower body. *The best way to condition your lower body for tennis is to maintain balance while you rehearse your strokes.* Jogging can develop endurance, sprinting can develop quickness, weight lifting can develop strength, but stroke rehearsal can develop all of these qualities while simultaneously programming muscle memory.

Jogging, sprinting, and weight lifting are effective ways to supplement practice, but they are only supplements. Actual stroke rehearsal is the best way to condition the necessary lower-body movements involved with preparing, executing, and recovering from one shot to the next. To condition your body for tennis, there is no substitute for the real thing.

▶

Get down: *Boris Becker's knees can't get much lower as he picks up this low backhand. This particular shot is too low for Becker not to flex at the waist as well as the knees.*

Use Your Eyes Effectively

When the loser of a recent U.S. Open match was asked to explain an uncharacteristic streak of errors, she responded, "I wasn't watching the ball." If her explanation is taken literally, it seems as silly as saying "I was holding the wrong end of the racket" or "I was trying to hit the ball *under* the net." The term *watch the ball* has become a cliché. Despite its vague and frequently inaccurate use, the term may be a part of our tennis vocabulary for some time to come.

"Watch the ball" is useful as a metaphor but not as a command to be taken literally. If someone advises you to "watch your step," it is unlikely that you will watch each and every one of your footsteps. "Watch your step" is a metaphor for exercising reasonable caution; "watch the ball" is a metaphor for using your eyes effectively.

In order to use your eyes effectively, you must see things clearly; in order to see things clearly, you must keep your head relatively stable in relation to the horizontal plane of the court. Vision provides information about the direction, speed, arc, and rotation of an approaching ball. If your head is bouncing up and down or turning from side to side, this visual information becomes distorted.

For a simple illustration of how visual acuity relates to head stability, notice the amount of effort required to read the words on this page. Now shake your head around as you read the next sentence. This is an example of a decrease in visual acuity due to the movement of your head. *All right, stop shaking your head.*

▶

Use your eyes: *Andre Agassi takes a good look before contact. Even if his eyes do not track the ball directly into the contact point, his head will remain stable.*

In addition to visual advantages, head stability also reinforces balance. Your head is a relatively heavy part of your body: if your head tilts forward, backward, or sideways, your upper body will tend to tilt with it. Unless you are forced to tilt your head due to the acceleration of your body, minimize head movement to maximize visual acuity and balance.

Using your eyes effectively means paying attention to the most relevant visual information. It is important to understand that the ball is not always the best source of information and that attempting to focus on the ball at every moment of its flight is counterproductive. Before your opponent hits the ball, it is not the ball, but your opponent's body that will provide the most relevant visual cues. As your opponent prepares to execute a stroke, the positions of his or her hips, shoulders, arm, and racket provide important information about the kind of shot that will be coming at you. It is only after your opponent's strings make contact with the ball that the ball itself provides the most relevant information.

Immediately before your opponent hits the ball, your eyes must scan your opponent for a quick assessment of the possibilities. Immediately after your opponent hits the ball, your eyes must scan the flight path of the approaching shot to ensure accurate contact. If your vision is clear, your eyes can perform these tasks with ease while simultaneously providing information about the location of the net, the location of your target, and your opponent's court position. Maintain head stability as you rehearse your strokes, and you may be surprised at what you see.

▶

Use your head: *Due to the rapid-fire nature of net play, even the best volleyers can get caught in ugly situations. Stefan Edberg's legs have failed him on this shot, but notice the upright position of his head and the symmetrical action of his arms. Head stability gives Edberg a chance to salvage the point.*

Establish a Consistent Contact Range

The contact point is that fraction of an inch where your strings make contact with the ball. The contact range is that area, relative to your body, where effective contact points are located. (The contact range usually provides more than one effective contact point.)

The ideal contact range for every stroke is located in front of your center of gravity: to a degree, the further in front, the greater the leverage. It is possible, however, to hit the ball too far in front. If you hit the ball too late or too early, the outcome will be a decrease in balance and leverage.

Due to variations in grip, stance, and backswing, the location of each stroke's contact range will vary slightly from one player to the next. However, in order to develop consistency for a particular stroke, that stroke's contact range must be consistent from one shot to the next. To maximize leverage, great players keep the contact range in front of the body's center of gravity, but not so far that balance is compromised.

The best way to find the most effective contact range for each stroke is to experiment during practice and realize that your own sense of balance and leverage is your best source of feedback. If your stroke feels crowded, you are probably hitting late. If you feel that you are leaning forward and losing balance, you are probably hitting too early. If you feel that you are hitting the ball with a balanced and efficient stroke, you are now hitting within an effective contact range.

▶

Hit in front: *Jim Courier makes contact almost a full arm's length in front of his body. If he tried to hit any further in front, he would have to lean or flex forward at the waist: this would cause a loss of balance. Since his body is not accelerating forward to intercept this shot, Courier maintains balance by keeping his upper body relatively vertical to the court.*

Swinging Strokes

The hips and shoulders are the central gears of the swing system. Therefore, the action of the muscles between the hips and shoulders is especially significant. An effective and efficient swing requires the balanced, integrated movement of many muscles throughout the body, but the swinging movement begins with the muscles of the trunk.

Most tennis players do not look exceptionally muscular. In fact, some of the game's hardest hitters could only be described as thin and lanky. When considering the physiques of great players, one may conclude that large amounts of muscular force are irrelevant and possibly detrimental to swinging a racket. Despite appearances, the most powerful swings require the largest amounts of muscular force.

Muscle is required to initiate hip and shoulder rotation, and more muscle is required to translate the force provided by that rotation into efficient racket movement. So if a high degree of muscular force is necessary for powerful shots, why aren't tennis players built like body builders, and why is it that your neighbor's thirteen-year-old daughter can hit the ball a hundred miles per hour? The answer lies in the distinction between the force provided by the contraction of muscle, and the force provided by the elastic action of muscle.

Generally speaking, the amount of contractile force that a muscle can exert is proportional to muscle mass. If, through training, the mass of a particular muscle increases, the amount of contractile force that the muscle can produce will increase as well. If, through inactivity, the mass of a particular muscle decreases, a decrease in contractile force will occur.

While all athletic events require a combination of contractile and elastic forces, some events require a relatively high degree of contractile force. In football, for example, a defensive lineman needs a high degree of contractile force to shove his way through the offensive line. A weight lifter needs a high degree of contractile force to execute a bench press, a dead lift, or a clean and jerk. Defensive linemen and weight lifters require exceptionally large amounts of muscle mass to produce the necessary contractile force to excel at their events. These athletes are undeniably strong, but their strength has little to do with producing a powerful tennis swing. When it comes to hitting a tennis ball, muscle elasticity is more significant than muscle mass.

▶

Stretch it: *Despite the long backswing, Becker keeps his racket in front of the plane of his shoulders. Note the plane of the hips in relation to the plane of the shoulders. At this phase of the swing, Becker is creating a stretch of the* trunk muscles, *not the arm muscles.*

Many athletic events demand relatively high degrees of elastic action. The force created by the elastic action of muscle is analogous to that of a rubber band being stretched and suddenly released. When a baseball pitcher throws a pitch, the forward rotation of his hips precedes the forward rotation of his shoulders. This "lag" between hip rotation and shoulder rotation will also occur when the batter swings his bat. This same phenomenon can be observed when a hockey player executes a slap shot, when a golfer hits a long drive, and—most important—when a tennis player takes a powerful swing. This lag creates a stretching in the muscles of the trunk (those muscles surrounding the athlete's center of gravity) followed by an explosive "snapping" motion of the shoulders.

It is important to note that increasing the total amount of hip and shoulder rotation will not necessarily increase the force of the swing. Too much rotation can negatively affect your timing and leverage. The amount of lag between the rotation of the hips and the rotation of the shoulders is a more important consideration than the total amount of rotation. Due to individual differences in flexibility, the exact amount of lag will vary from one player to the next. Regardless of your flexibility, your most forceful swings will occur only when you have achieved an effective stretch of the resisting trunk muscles.

The actions of lagging, stretching, and snapping are not limited to the hips, shoulders, and trunk. The progression of force from the body's center of gravity to the racket head is a coordinated series of lags, stretches, and snaps. This progression is most visible during the service motion: the shoulders snap after lagging behind the hips; the elbow snaps after lagging behind the shoulders; the wrist snaps after lagging behind the elbow; and finally, the racket head whips through after lagging behind the wrist.

Rotate back: *Cedric Pioline rotates his hips and shoulders away from the target as he tosses the ball. Note the slight, rotational stretch between the plane of the hips and the plane of the shoulders.*

Rotate forward: *Pioline's hips and shoulders begin to rotate forward before the racket head drops to the farthest point of the backswing. This creates a powerful stretch of the shoulder and arm muscles.*

Snap: *After the muscles of the trunk and arm have done their work, Pioline's wrist snap is the final, explosive action before contact.*

USE ELASTICITY

If the concept of elasticity is new to you, the following experiment may help you gain an appreciation of how the elastic action of muscle relates to the force of a swing.

First, place your racket in a backswing position as if you are about to hit a forehand groundstroke. Keep your shoulder, elbow, and wrist relatively stiff and swing several times at a moderate speed. For this group of swings, use only hip and shoulder rotation to provide racket movement: your racket and hitting shoulder should move as a solid unit, like a door on a hinge.

Now take several more swings using a comparable speed of hip and shoulder rotation, but loosen your shoulder, elbow, and wrist and allow the racket head to lag behind momentarily at the instant you begin your shoulder rotation: make the lag as brief as possible. During this group of swings, you should feel an increase in racket-head speed; you may be able to hear the difference as the racket swishes through the air.

Finally, swing the racket a few more times, but instead of simply allowing the racket to lag momentarily, actually move the racket back slightly as you begin to rotate your shoulders forward. In other words, instead of starting your racket movement from a stationary position, complete your backswing a split second *after* hip and shoulder rotation begins. With the arm and racket turning in one direction, and the shoulders turning in the opposite direction, you should feel a slight stretch followed by a quick burst of racket-head speed.

▶

Lag a little: *The backward rotation of Pete Sampras's right shoulder is almost complete, but the racket movement lags behind. By the time his racket completes the backswing, the shoulders will have already started to rotate forward.*

ESTABLISH A BASE OF SUPPORT

Your feet, in contact with the court, provide the primary leverage for hip and shoulder rotation. As force progresses from
the trunk outward through the arms, it also progresses downward through the legs. Therefore, it is not uncommon that
the force of the swing will lift one or both of your feet off
the ground during forward rotation. While you may find yourself leaving the ground at some point during a swing, it is critical that you plant one or both of your feet just prior to
rotation. Even in situations in which you are forced to leap
into the air to reach a ball, most of the leverage for your swing
is dependent on the position of your feet prior to jumping.

If you have any doubts about the importance of planting
the feet, jump in the air and try to quickly rotate your hips
and shoulders while your feet are off the ground. Now try
rotating your hips and shoulders while your feet are planted
approximately shoulder width apart. This comparison should
clearly indicate which condition provides the best balance and
leverage for an effective rotation to occur.

When you execute a swing, your feet have a second purpose as well: they provide a base of support for weight transfer. However, maintaining balance and creating force with hip
and shoulder rotation is more important than achieving a high
degree of weight transfer on swinging strokes. Many recreational players overemphasize weight transfer to the extent
that it inhibits balance, rotation, and recovery. Relax and let

◄

Stretch for power: *The forward rotation of Sampras's shoulders begins*
before *the racket has completed its backward movement. This creates a*
stretch and snap of the arm muscles.

your weight transfer naturally as you swing. On shots such as the overhead smash, you may have no choice but to move your body weight in the opposite direction of your target; even moving backward, you can still hit a very powerful shot. Trust your own sense of balance to tell you when and how to transfer weight on swinging strokes.

▶

Go with the flow: *The explosive progression of force from his center of gravity outward sends Courier's feet flying.*

THE FOREHAND GROUNDSTROKE

When the racket head moves into the backswing position for the forehand groundstroke, the plane of the shoulders is turned sideways to the target. At the completion of the forward swing, the plane of the shoulders faces the target. The shoulders will rotate approximately 90 degrees when taking a full swing on the forehand.

Remembering the term *90 degrees* will also remind you of effective racket and forearm position for the stroke. Just prior to the forward rotation of your shoulders, your forearm will form an angle of approximately 90 degrees with the plane of your shoulders. Likewise, your racket will form an angle of approximately 90 degrees with your forearm. These two 90-degree angles will be present at the contact point as well.

The next four photographs and the accompanying text will illustrate how the term *90 degrees* can help you develop proper forehand fundamentals.

▶

90 degrees: *With his forearm at a 90-degree angle to the plane of his shoulders and his racket at a 90-degree angle to his forearm, Michael Chang will rotate his shoulders 90 degrees before contact.*

Lock In

Just as the forward rotation of the shoulders begins, the wrist locks into a laid-back position, and the elbow is bent and locked into position slightly in front of the torso. The locked-in positions of the wrist and elbow are almost identical to their positions at the point of contact.

Regardless of stance or type of backswing, all good forehands lock in. Straight backswings lock in early, while looped backswings lock in relatively late, usually an instant after the forward rotation of the shoulders begins. Locking in early decreases the amount of stretch in the arm muscles and provides a relatively slow but consistent racket-head speed; this in turn creates a relatively long contact range. Locking in late provides a greater muscular stretch, which provides a more explosive swing.

If you want a smoother, flatter shot with a longer contact range, lock in earlier, but be prepared for a decrease in racket-head speed. If you want to add pace or spin to your forehand, lock in later.

▶

Lock in: *Before initiating a powerful rotation of the hips and shoulders, Sampras positions his hand and racket head in front of the plane of his shoulders. His right elbow is away from his body, but it will lock into position as the racket head loops down.*

Lock in: *Like Sampras in the previous photo, Steffi Graf takes a high backswing with the racket parallel to the plane of her shoulders. Before her racket reaches the contact point, the racket head will swoop down below the level of contact. This creates a rotational stretch of the forearm, which, in turn, provides an explosive burst of racket-head speed.*

Lock in: *Courier's racket and forearm form a perfect right angle. At this phase of the swing, the muscles of his trunk have stretched and snapped, and the tip of his racket has lagged slightly behind the plane of the shoulders. Note how his right elbow locks into position before contact.*

Face It

Time your rotation so that contact occurs as the plane of your shoulders faces the target. If you rotate too soon, the racket will drag too far behind the shoulders. If you rotate too late, the muscles of the shoulder, arm, and wrist will have to provide most of the force. In both cases, your racket will be out of sync with the force provided by the elastic action of your trunk.

Facing the target at the moment of contact creates two effective outcomes. First, it allows you to initiate an effective hip and shoulder rotation before contact. Second, moving your hitting shoulder forward creates the best overall position for hitting the ball in front of your center of gravity.

Time your rotation, make contact in front of your center of gravity, and *face it* . . . it works.

▶

Face it: *Note the similarity between the wrist position of Courier's contact point and his locked-in wrist position in the previous photo.*

Face it: *Conchita Martinez demonstrates good balance and a well-timed hip and shoulder rotation. At contact, her upper body faces the target, and she hits the ball in front of her center of gravity.*

Face it: *After contact, Agassi's right shoulder finishes slightly in front of his left shoulder. The elbow "disconnects" from the locked-in position as the racket drives through the ball.*

THE ONE-HANDED BACKHAND

When the racket head is at the farthest point of the backswing for the one-handed backhand, the hitting shoulder rotates so that the back of the shoulder blade faces the target. Concentrate on the position of the hitting shoulder only; if you try to turn the back of both shoulder blades to the target, you will not be able to turn your head enough to see the approaching ball. At the contact point, the plane of the shoulders should form a line to the target. The hitting shoulder will rotate approximately 90 degrees when taking a full swing on the backhand groundstroke.

The next seven photographs and the accompanying text will illustrate how you can reinforce proper one-handed backhand fundamentals by controlling the movement of the hitting shoulder.

▶

Wind it up: *Shoulder tucked under chin, elbow down, Becker winds up for a topspin backhand. Note the plane of the hips in relation to the plane of the shoulders: at this phase of the swing, Becker is stretching the trunk muscles.*

Tuck It In

At the completion of the backswing, the lead shoulder is tucked under the chin and the elbow remains below shoulder level. The tucked-in backswing is a staple of practically all good one-handed backhands. (The only exception is flat, or under-spin, strokes played above shoulder level: for these shots, it is necessary to raise the elbow.)

With your eyes on the ball, rotate the hitting shoulder so the back of the shoulder blade faces the ball. Rotating your shoulder during preparation establishes your source of power. If you don't tuck in the shoulder, you will not achieve an effective stretch of the trunk muscles, and your wrist and arm will have to provide all the force. This results in a loss of power and control. Tuck in as early as possible, pick your target, and prepare to unleash your swing.

▶

Tuck it in: *Poised, balanced, and relaxed, Sampras demonstrates a classic, tucked-in backswing. His shoulder is tucked under his chin, the back of his shoulder blade faces his target, and the racket head has broken the plane of his shoulders.*

Tuck it in: *Like Sampras in the previous photo, Martina Navratilova tucks her hitting shoulder under her chin. Since the approaching ball is higher than the one Sampras is about to hit, she raises her elbow in preparation for a high slice.*

Tuck it in: *Like most two-handed backhand players, Sanchez-Vicario switches to one hand for slices. If she were using a two-handed stroke, the hitting shoulder would not rotate this far back and the racket head would not break the plane of the shoulders.*

The Back Blast

Anyone who has seen old war movies is familiar with the way a bazooka fires. As the projectile shoots from the front of the barrel, a simultaneous blast emits from the back of the barrel. This "back blast" counters the force of the projectile and prevents the person who pulled the trigger from being knocked backward.

For a one-handed backhand, the nonracket arm is as functional as it is for the two-handed backhand. For the one-handed stroke, however, the arms do not move in the same direction. Think of the nonracket arm as the back blast that counters the force of the racket. As the racket arm moves in the direction of the target, the nonracket arm moves simultaneously in the opposite direction. In other words, for the action of the racket arm, there is an opposite reaction of the nonracket arm.

The back blast helps keep the shoulders from overrotating, thus allowing the racket to move in a direct line to the target. Remember to keep your shoulders sideways to the target as you use the back blast, and you will be on your way to a bazooka backhand.

▶

Back blast: *The movement of his left hand keeps Sampras's hitting shoulder in front of his body. The plane of his shoulders is sideways to the target at contact.*

Back blast: *Although his body weight is moving rapidly to the side of the court, Yannick Noah maintains balance during the follow-through. Noah has moved both arms simultaneously in opposite directions.*

Back blast: *The balance provided by her left hand will help Graf recover from this wide backhand.*

THE TWO-HANDED BACKHAND

The greatest advantage of the two-handed backhand is that you can make contact with the ball relatively close to your body and still produce a powerful, controlled shot. When the approaching ball gets too close to the one-handed player, he or she must use underspin in order to maintain control. A two-handed player, however, can maintain control over this same shot while ripping through it with a powerful topspin. This advantage alone is enough to convince some players that two hands are better than one.

The greatest disadvantage of using two hands is that it limits your range and variety. Gripping the racket with both hands inhibits balance on wide shots, low shots, underspin shots, and shots that require you to move through the stroke (see Chapter 5). It is no coincidence that all of the great serve-and-volleyers throughout history have used one-handed backhands: quite simply, the two-hander is a less versatile stroke. Does this mean that the one-hander is the better stroke? Yes, if your definition of *better* is "more versatile." No, if your definition is "more pace and topspin."

If you are a two-hander and have exceptional footwork, you may be able to avoid situations that will put the stroke at a disadvantage. But if you are like most players who use a two-handed backhand, you will switch to a one-handed stroke for volleys, underspins, and shots requiring extra reach.

There is a significant difference in hip and shoulder rotation between the two-handed and one-handed backhands. Hip and shoulder rotation for the two-handed stroke is similar to rotation for the forehand groundstroke. Before the forward rotation of the shoulders begins, the wrists and elbows lock into a position that approximates their position at the point of contact. The shoulders rotate to face the target when contact occurs. *Lock in* on the backswing, *face it* on the contact point, and *rip through it* to take advantage of the extra pace and topspin that the stroke provides.

Face it: *Some of my students tell me they prefer a two-handed backhand over a one-handed backhand because the two-handed stroke feels like a forehand. Courier's groundstrokes illustrate this point. Compare this shot with the forehand shot on page 49.*

Lock in: *Seles keeps the plane of the racket head parallel to the plane of her shoulders during preparation for this two-handed stroke. The plane of her shoulders will rotate to face her target on the follow-through.*

Face it: *Seles's right elbow disconnects from the locked-in position after her shoulders rotate forward. It is as if she were hitting a one-handed forehand with her right hand (she is left-handed).*

THE SERVE

During the service motion, the progression of force from the body's center of gravity to the racket head is almost identical to an overhand throwing motion. An effective throwing motion uses a stretch and snap of the trunk muscles and a whipping motion of the arm. If you can throw a ball effectively, notice the position of your hips and shoulders at the beginning and end of your throwing motion and try to duplicate those positions when serving.

If you can't throw a ball effectively, supplement your serving practice with some throwing practice. Stand at the baseline and throw balls high above the net to the opposite side of the court. Maintain balance, concentrate on leading with the hips to achieve an effective stretch of the trunk muscles, and use your arm like a whip to transfer the power provided by hip and shoulder rotation. Remember that achieving an extremely high degree of hip and shoulder rotation is not as significant as achieving an effective stretch of the resisting trunk muscles.

The next two sections will illustrate how you can reinforce proper serving fundamentals by focusing on a balanced hip and shoulder rotation and the whipping motion of the arm.

▶

Heads up: *When the ball leaves her tossing hand, the tip of Graf's racket points up. A common error is to point the racket head down and behind the back at this phase of the swing; this prevents an effective stretch of the shoulder and arm muscles.*

Turn and Flex

The turn-and-flex position occurs at the end of the tossing
motion; it is the starting point for the forward rotation of
your hips and shoulders. "Turn" refers to your hips and shoulders turning away from your target prior to an explosive, forward rotation. "Flex" refers to the position of your knees and
hitting elbow.

It is true that flexing and extending the knees can acceler-
ate hip rotation and subsequently add pace to your serve.
However, too much knee flexion can cause a loss of balance
and timing. Due to individual differences in strength and flexibility, the appropriate degree of knee flexion will vary from
one player to the next. Stay balanced and relaxed, and you
will find the amount of knee flexion that is right for you.
Remember that maintaining balance is more important than
achieving a high degree of knee flexion.

When you are turned, flexed, and ready to unleash your
swing, the tip of your racket is *not* pointing down. Just as if
you were throwing the racket, your elbow will whip up and
the racket will snap down behind your back as you initiate
the forward rotation of your shoulders.

▶

Turn and flex: *Sampras rotates back with the hitting shoulder as he
flexes the knees and bends the hitting elbow. In addition to controlling
the toss, the high tossing hand assists in the positioning of the upper
body.*

Turn and flex: *Lendl pauses momentarily with the racket in a straight-up position. This feeling of balancing the racket can help ensure that the hitting arm is appropriately relaxed and ready to initiate a whipping motion.*

Turn and flex: *While John McEnroe's service motion has produced exceptional results, most players would find it difficult to maintain balance when turning this far away from the target and flexing the knees this much. McEnroe is more extreme than most players in many respects.*

Snap the Whip

Imagine snapping a whip. The force that results in the snapping action originates from your body, not the whip itself. Likewise, your hitting arm is not the primary source of power for the serve. Use your arm like a whip: an object that transfers and focuses the power initiated by the stretch and snap of your trunk muscles.

For your arm to be an effective whip, the muscles of the arm must remain loose as the elbow drives up to the ball. Just as if you were throwing the racket, the elbow snaps up as the racket head snaps down behind your back. In this way, the snapping motion of the forearm and racket will be the final, explosive actions before contact.

The movements leading up to the turn-and-flex position should be smooth and slow; this is where a natural pause in the motion will occur. Think of the turn and flex as the calm before the storm. Snapping the whip, on the other hand, is an instantaneous sequence: let your legs extend as your hips rotate, feel the stretch as the shoulders rotate, and let shoulder rotation initiate the whipping motion of the arm.

▶

Snap the whip: *Lendl's racket snaps down his back as his hitting shoulder begins to snap up to the ball. His feet leave the ground as a result of force progressing downward through the legs.*

Snap the whip: *Sampras keeps his feet on the court until the whipping motion of his arm has been initiated. His left elbow drops as his right elbow drives up to the ball: this motion of the arms is indicative of a synchronized rotation around a balanced axis.*

Snap the whip: *During the turn-and-flex position, Seles's right elbow was positioned above her shoulders and her left elbow was below her shoulders. Here, an instant before contact, her elbows have "see-sawed." The force initiated by her trunk muscles is now being translated into racket-head speed.*

THE OVERHEAD SMASH

Most errors on the overhead smash can be attributed to poor positioning. Poor positioning, in turn, can be attributed to the fact that lobs are the easiest shots to misjudge, especially in windy or sunny conditions. It is not unusual to make last-second positioning adjustments in order to hit an effective smash.

A quick, consistent preparation sequence is critical for ensuring good position. As soon as your opponent lobs, *turn sideways* and *back up*. When you turn sideways, place your racket and hitting arm in the same position as for the turn and flex (see page 68). Remember to keep the tip of the racket pointing up to maximize the whipping action of the arm.

Turning sideways establishes your source of power and makes it easier to move back for the shot. Backing up is critical, because if you misjudge the oncoming lob, it is better to be too far behind the ball than to have the ball too far behind you. It is easier to make any last-second positioning adjustments while moving forward instead of backward.

▶

Extend up: *Becker begins an explosive upward movement to the ball. Note the similarity of his body position on this shot and the body positions illustrated on pages 73, 74, and 75.*

When executing your swing, *extend up* to the contact point, and *snap through* with the wrist. Contact at full extension provides maximum racket-head velocity and maximum net clearance. The ideal trajectory for the overhead depends on your height and court position: if you are six feet tall and positioned three feet away from the net, the downward angle can be much greater than if you are five feet tall and positioned at the service line. Experiment during practice to find the trajectory that will provide maximum effectiveness.

It is important to remember that there are situations in which an overhead motion is appropriate, but a smash is inappropriate. For example, if you are hitting an overhead from very deep in your court, "smashing" the ball at full force will often send it into the net or the back fence. The farther you are from the net, the narrower your margin of error. Unless you have great confidence in your swing or you are a reckless gambler, take it easy when your opponent makes a very deep lob. If you are far away from the net when hitting the overhead, swing at three-quarter speed and use enough spin to ensure that the ball will clear the net and drop into the court.

▶

Snap through: *Ivanisevic extends up with the arm and snaps through with the wrist. Due to the height of his racket at contact and his position on the court, Ivanisevic can drive this ball on a downward angle.*

The Backhand Overhead

Most errors on the backhand overhead occur from trying to overpower the shot. It can be difficult to maintain balance and leverage when the backhand is stretched to an extreme height, and this makes it difficult to generate force.

Unless your opponent is severely out of position, or the approaching lob is so short that you can angle the overhead for a winner, a deep placement shot is the most practical option.

If the approaching lob is high enough, step around the shot and play a regular overhead on the forehand side. The forehand side will always provide more explosive options for the overhead.

Tuck in during the backswing as you would for a backhand groundstroke, but use the additional cue *elbow up, racket head down*. If you don't raise the elbow, you will feel strain in the hitting shoulder as you begin the swing. *Back blast* with the nonracket arm to help maintain balance and drive the racket head through the contact range.

▶

Back blast: *Marc Rosset separates his hands as the racket moves forward. Although he is in midair and reaching up for a relatively difficult shot, he is able to stay poised and balanced by using both the left and right halves of his body to execute the stroke.*

Punching Strokes

The mechanics of punching strokes seem simple enough to be taken for granted. This may explain why they are the most neglected strokes at every level of the sport.

An efficient punching stroke uses compact, precise movements. The time required to prepare, execute, and recover from a punching stroke is significantly less than from a swinging stroke. Punches are more reliable than swings when your opponent blasts a powerful serve or overhead that forces you to make a quick-reflex response. A punching stroke may also be needed as a result of your court position: there are few times when you will approach the net and not have to use a punching stroke.

A punching stroke is a controlled, simultaneous thrust of the racket and the body weight. The movement of your racket head should be *short* and *direct*: short, because the shortest distance between two points is a straight line; direct, because that line should be directed to your target. The most common error that occurs during a punching stroke is moving the racket in a circular, indirect path around the body—in other words, swinging too much. Remember that your form is likely to loosen during a match; if you allow a slight swing during practice, you may swing even more under match conditions. If, however, you rehearse your strokes using a strict punching form, a slight loosening of form during a match should not be too detrimental.

In order to hit consistently effective shots during quick-reflex situations, you must learn to rely on a simple stroke. A simple stroke begins with a compact preparation. Three cues will help you accomplish this.

First, *keep your hand in front* of your center of gravity as you make the initial move to the ball. Instead of thinking of your preparation as a backswing, think of it as an alignment of the racket face. During this alignment, most of the racket movement is produced by the wrist, not the arm or trunk. Use your wrist to align your racket face to the target during preparation and maintain that alignment even after contact (see photos of Jimmy Connors, Bjorn Borg, and Javier Sanchez on pages 87, 92, and 93, respectively).

The second cue to help simplify your preparation is *accuracy first, power second*. A powerful volley that bounces too short, for example, is not as effective as a medium-paced volley hit deep into the corner. Don't worry about hitting a powerful shot until you are sure you can place the ball where you want it to go. Big backswings and wild shots are usually the result of attempting to hit the ball too hard.

The third preparation cue is *tilt the racket head*. All punching strokes require some degree of underspin to control the flight of the ball. It is important to remember that underspin is created by the angle of the racket head on contact, not the direction of racket movement. If your racket head is angled with a slight upward tilt at contact, you will produce underspin even if your racket remains perfectly motionless. It is also important to remember that a minor change in the angle of the racket head can produce a major change in the flight of the ball. Experiment during practice and adjust the angle of the racket a few degrees at a time until you find the desired depth for your shot.

While the racket movement of a punching stroke is relatively limited, sufficient force for the shot can be generated by weight transfer and the thrusting motion of the arm.

Weight transfer is the most significant source of power for punching strokes, and a balanced weight transfer requires foot movement. An important cue for your lower body is *time the step*. As you thrust your racket to the ball, step forward with your opposite foot (if the shot is to your left, step with the right foot; if the shot is to your right, step with the left foot). If your foot touches the court before your strings hit the ball, you will have exhausted your weight transfer. Rehearse the timing of your step so that your foot touches the court at the same moment that your strings hit the ball.

As you rehearse your strokes, remember that using weight transfer does not mean that you have to lunge or lean into the stroke. Make your move aggressively but not at the expense of balance. A balanced weight transfer helps you achieve effective racket-head control during the stroke and efficient recovery after the stroke. Unless the position of the approaching ball forces you to lunge, use a balanced weight transfer by keeping your upper body perpendicular to the court.

Thrust your racket to the ball as you step into the stroke. Move your hand forward on a line parallel to the movement of your racket head. If the racket head hinges in a circular path around the wrist, the angle of the racket face will change at every point of its movement. When the racket head, hand, and wrist move parallel to each other, the angle of the racket face will stay aligned to the target throughout the stroke.

There is no question that a hinging or snapping motion of the wrist can add substantial pace to your shot, but there are two reasons to be cautious of this technique. First, the hinging action of the wrist will shorten your contact range and decrease accuracy. Second, relying on a wrist snap may cause you to neglect footwork, and as footwork goes, so go your punching strokes. Before resorting to a wrist snap, make sure you have established a consistent and accurate punching stroke that makes the most out of your weight transfer; then consider if additional pace is necessary for your level of competition.

Placement is a punching stroke's main weapon. In a quick-reflex situation, common sense tells you not to take a big swing, but a desire to hit the ball hard may tell you otherwise. If you remember that weight transfer and the thrusting motion of the arm provide sufficient force for a punching stroke, you will learn to respond to both voices: the one that says "Don't swing," and the one that screams "Win the point!"

▶

Short and direct: *Jimmy Connors aligns his racket face to the target before contact. Note the position of his feet and the obvious, forward thrust of his body weight. At this phase of the stroke, he is in the process of transferring weight.*

THE BOUNCE STEP

A bounce step increases your ability to make quick, explosive movements to intercept an approaching ball. While this ability is important for all strokes (except the serve), it is especially critical for punching strokes. A punching stroke is used in place of a swing when you have relatively little time to execute your stroke. If you are not currently using the bounce step, punching strokes are the best place to start using it.

The bounce step is a simple movement: with your feet approximately shoulder-width apart, flex and extend the knees in a springing action as you lift your heels off the ground. The flexion of the knees is not extreme, nor is the extension a complete extension. Imagine that you are playing hopscotch and you are about to hop onto a block with both feet. The bounce step is a similar movement, but you are bouncing up and down instead of forward.

Maintaining balance during the bounce step is critical, because at the instant you execute the movement, you don't know where your opponent's shot is headed. If you bounce in one direction or another in an attempt to guess the flight path of your opponent's shot, you will decrease your ability to move in the opposite direction. Bounce-step at approximately the same time your opponent makes contact with the ball, and maintain balance by moving your body weight straight up and down.

Bounce step is an appropriate term because of the similarity between a ball bouncing on the court, and the body springing into action. A ball compresses when it hits the court and decompresses when it rises. Likewise, your body compresses when the knees flex, and decompresses when the knees extend. When your body decompresses, your body weight literally decreases, thus the expression, "light on your feet."

The trick to using the bounce step for punching strokes is timing that instant of decompression with your awareness of

Bounce step: *Knees flexed, upper body vertical to the court, McEnroe prepares to spring into action. An instant after his feet hit the ground, he will begin to move to the approaching ball.*

the approaching ball's direction; in other words, you should be bouncing up as you make your move to the ball. This timing can be acquired through a simple volley drill. Stand at net position and have your practice partner feed random shots to your forehand and backhand sides. Bounce-step just as your partner makes contact, then turn your hips and move with the opposite foot when you recognize whether the shot is a forehand or backhand.

LOW VOLLEYS

For the sake of simplifying your net strategy, divide your volleys into two categories: low volleys and high volleys. High volleys may use a synthesis of weight transfer and a swinging motion, while low volleys require a strict punching motion. (High volleys will be discussed in Chapter 5.)

The line which divides a low volley from a high volley is a relative one. As an individual player, you must decide when a volley is so low that it must be punched. For example, if you are positioned at the service line and you are faced with a volley at the exact height of the net, will you execute a punch, or will you risk a swing? If you like to maximize pace, you will probably swing. If you rely on placement and variety, you will probably punch. If, however, you don't have the slightest idea what to do in this situation, I strongly recommend that you punch. A punch is the safest option, and you must learn to play it safe before you learn to gamble.

A good rule is to punch any volley below net level. If the ball is near the exact height of the net and you have any doubt whatsoever, punch it. Good volleyers seldom second-guess themselves. The first step to mastering volleys is knowing when the ball is too low to risk a swing.

For low volleys, the ball *must* be hit in a slight arc to avoid the net. The obvious difficulty is hitting in an arc high enough to ensure accuracy, but not so high that it gives your opponent an easy option to win the point. In tennis terms, you must avoid blasting it out, dumping it into the net, or floating it back and getting burned with a passing shot.

A good cue for controlling the low volley is *drive forward*. A slight downward movement of the racket is often necessary to control the arc of the ball, but make sure that most of the movement is forward. There are two common errors on the low volley: trying to lift the ball over by "scooping" up with the racket, or trying to spin the ball over by "chopping" down. Both circumstances invite poor balance and all its related disadvantages. Trust the upward tilt of your racket head to provide enough arc for your shot to clear the net; scooping or chopping is unnecessary.

The exact upward tilt depends on your court position and the height of the approaching ball. As you rehearse your low volley, experiment with the upward tilt of your racket head, maintain balance, and drive *forward* with the racket, not up or down.

Time the step: *Bjorn Borg's strings make contact with the ball as his front foot makes contact with the court. (Note the identical timing of the volleys in the photos on pages 8 and 9.)*

Drive forward: *Javier Sanchez keeps a firm wrist and maintains alignment of the racket face until the end of the follow-through. Note that the plane of his shoulders is sideways to his target; he is able to maintain this shoulder position with the assistance of his left arm.*

LEARN TO LOVE THE BACKHAND VOLLEY

The following situation may seem familiar: you hit your first volley too short and give your opponent a floater, which he or she tries to blast right through your body. In situations like this, where you must switch from offense to self-defense, the point can be saved by committing to the backhand volley.

When the approaching shot is headed directly at your navel, a backhand volley is much easier to execute than a forehand. If you commit to the backhand side and find that you have misjudged the position of the approaching ball, it is still possible to play an effective backhand volley even if the ball is slightly to the forehand side. The forehand volley does not offer the same versatility. If you attempt forehand volleys in situations where the ball is fired directly into your body, you will usually find yourself jammed to the point of ineffectiveness.

When you are attacked at the net, *defend with a backhand*. Step into the shot if you have time to do so. If there is no time to step, turn the shoulders so that the hitting shoulder is in front of your center of gravity. If there is no time to turn the shoulders, simply get the strings on the ball and deflect it back over the net.

▶

Defend with the backhand: *Gabriela Sabatini drops the racket head to deflect a backhand into the open court. The follow-through finishes on the forehand side, but contact is made with the backhand side of the racket.*

Defend with the backhand: *The ball crowds Ivanisevic on this forehand volley, and his elbow drifts behind his torso. This severely limits his arm's range of motion. Note that he has become relatively flat-footed as his upper body tilts away from the shot.*

Defend with the backhand: *On the backhand volley, Ivanisevic's elbow stays in front of his torso; this gives his arm a greater range of motion. For this shot, Ivanisevic is lighter on his feet and will be able to regain his balance much faster.*

SERVICE RETURN

Use a punching stroke to return serve when your opponent is serving with overwhelming pace or spin. Of course, the definition of an overwhelming serve is relative. If you can return serve effectively with a swing, go ahead and tee off. However, if you are losing two or more points per game because you fail to get the serve back into play (even if the serve is not so overwhelming), reduce your swing and start punching.

An effective punched return is seldom an outright winner, nor is it a purely defensive shot. The function of this stroke is to neutralize the serve and prevent your opponent from taking control of the point.

Placement is a punched return's main weapon. The best placement depends on your opponent's style of offense. If your opponent serves and volleys, a low trajectory is critical. If your opponent stays back after serving, depth is your primary concern. In both cases, create a pattern of guiding the ball to your opponent's weak side, and throw in variations to keep your opponent off balance.

▶

Close in: *McEnroe steps in to block a return. He is limiting his opponent's offensive possibilities in two ways. First, he is controlling the direction and trajectory of the return. Second, his compact, balanced follow-through will allow him to recover from this stroke and move explosively for the next one.*

The Half-Volley

The half-volley is one of the most demanding challenges of a player's timing. When you are executing a half-volley, you have an extremely short distance between the bounce and the contact point. This creates the unique problem of estimating when contact will occur. Because the distance between the bounce and the contact point is so short, there is no time to make adjustments after the ball has bounced. The estimation of the contact point is based entirely on the speed, spin, and trajectory of the ball *before* it has hit the court.

All good half-volleyers have an instinctual hierarchy for dealing with half-volley situations. The following is a simple hierarchy that will help guide the necessary reflexes for the half-volley.

▶

Short and direct: *Becker keeps the racket head in front of his center of gravity as he prepares to push the racket forward.*

Best Option: *Avoid the half-volley.* Adjust your court position if you have time to do so. Step forward and play a punched volley; or step back, let the ball bounce and rise, and use a short swing. If you have time to choose, eliminate the option of the half-volley.

Second-Best Option: *When a half-volley is inevitable, use a short swing.* If you are caught off balance or out of position, a half-volley may be your only choice. When you have time to prepare, but not enough time to reposition and choose a safer option, use a short swing. This will provide the greatest penetration for your shot.

Last Option: *Use a punching stroke.* If you have moved forward in an attempt to hit a low volley, but the ball bounces before you reach it, a punching stroke is your only option. In this situation, your racket is in front of your center of gravity and you have already started your weight transfer. Keep your wrist firm, time your step, and punch for depth. A drop shot is a reasonable alternative for this situation, but use it sparingly. Your opponent may move into the court when he or she sees that you are forced to half-volley; a drop shot must be extremely precise when your opponent sees it coming.

▶

Drive forward: *McEnroe keeps a firm wrist as he drives forward, not downward, on the half-volley.*

Combined Strokes

Hip and shoulder rotation is the most significant source of power for swinging strokes. Weight transfer is the most significant source of power for punching strokes. When you use an almost equal combination of both sources, you are executing a combined stroke.

When is it necessary to combine weight transfer and a swinging motion? Whenever two conditions are present: you are moving forward as you hit the ball, and the shot requires more force than a punching stroke can provide. Approach shots and high volleys usually require a combined stroke.

Think of a combined stroke as a swing supplemented by weight transfer. Use the same footwork that you would use for a punching stroke: step with the opposite foot and time the step so that you are in the process of weight transfer as your strings make contact with the ball. Because the weight transfer supplements the power of the swing, a full swing is usually unnecessary.

Regulate the length of your swing by the amount of weight transfer that your forward movement provides. If you are running at full speed to reach an opponent's drop shot, the swing should be extremely short because your momentum will provide a naturally high degree of weight transfer. Conversely, if you are only taking one step forward to increase your angle for a high volley, a slightly longer swing is necessary because the force of your weight transfer is not as great.

A good cue for combined strokes is *increase your footwork, decrease your backswing.* Increasing the amount of footwork helps ensure that you don't simply lean or stretch to reach the ball. Decreasing the backswing will increase accuracy and simplify your timing.

TWO APPROACHES TO THE APPROACH SHOT

There are two basic techniques for hitting approach shots: stopping and planting the feet before hitting the shot, or moving through the shot. Planting the feet maximizes the forcefulness of the approach shot itself; moving through the approach shot maximizes the effectiveness of your subsequent net position.

The advantage of planting the feet is obvious: balance, timing, and an effective stretch of the trunk muscles are all easier to achieve from a stable base, and this makes it easier to cut loose with your stroke. The disadvantage of this technique is that once you have planted your feet, cutting loose is your

▶

Cut loose: *Sanchez tears into an approach shot. The long swing will slow down his attack.*

only option. Because stopping and restarting your movement creates a pause in your transition, you may not be able to close in on the net fast enough to intercept a passing shot. Hitting a devastating approach shot is the major key to success for this strategy.

If you move through the approach shot, however, you will be able to close in quickly and significantly reduce the targets for your opponent's passing shots. With this technique, there is less pressure on the approach shot itself, and this is critical to your entire attack strategy. If you feel uncomfortable attacking behind anything less than a devastating approach shot, you may find yourself stranded at the baseline. Moving through the approach shot makes a successful attack possible off any moderately short ball: an easy setup from your opponent is not required.

While moving through the approach shot is the more versatile technique, don't rely on it as your exclusive means of approaching the net. The ability to use both techniques forces your opponent to respond to two radically different passing situations; this alone can cause confusion for your opponent. When you have the opportunity to plant your feet, simply shorten your backswing and use your normal cues for a swinging stroke. When you don't have time to plant your feet, you must be able to move through the approach, and this is when it is necessary to synthesize elements of the punch and the swing.

▶

Combine sources: *Novotna makes a smooth, solid approach by combining power sources. By moving through the shot, she will reach the net faster than Sanchez will.*

THE HIGH VOLLEY

When you approach the net and your opponent hits a high return, you will usually have two options: close in and volley the ball while it is still high, or wait until the ball reaches you and settle for a lower volley. While some strokes are best to avoid (like the half-volley and the backhand overhead), the high volley is a stroke that should be used whenever you have the opportunity. When hitting a high volley, the net becomes less of an obstacle for your shot; therefore, it is possible to drive the ball with considerably more pace than a low volley.

Three important reasons dictate moving into the high volley: first, to provide the force of weight transfer; second, to increase the range of possible angles for your shot; and third, to make sure that you reach the ball before it drops below net height. In a high-volley situation, *close in* quickly and *attack the ball*. When it comes to volleys, he who hesitates must be ready for low shots.

▶

Punch when it's low: *Krajicek keeps the racket movement short and direct on this low volley. Compare this follow-through with the high volley on page 113.*

Use a short swing for the high volley, instead of simply punching the shot, in order to add velocity. Compared to the low volley, the high volley is more of a line drive, and less of a parabola. This means that your shot can reach its target fast enough to result in an outright winner. Of course, a swing isn't always necessary; if your opponent is severely out of position, simply punch the ball into the open court.

When hitting high volleys, remember to increase your footwork and decrease your backswing. Move through the shot to provide weight transfer and pay particular attention to driving the racket head forward instead of downward. Because the ball is above the level of the net, aiming down can be very tempting, but this will usually send your shot into the net. Drive the racket head forward to avoid the net and to maximize the pace and depth of your shot.

▶

Swing when it's high: *McEnroe swings through as he steps into this high volley.*

Attack the ball: *The author goes after a high backhand volley.*

Drive forward: *Keep a firm wrist as you drive through the high backhand volley.*

Afterword

I hope this book has inspired you to practice your strokes with renewed enthusiasm. You may want to customize some of the cues to make them more personally significant or memorable. Make your stroke cues simple and be sure you have defined a clear and specific action that they reinforce.

If you want to improve more than one stroke and you are not sure where to begin, start with your weakest stroke. The stroke that players avoid the most is usually the stroke that they need to practice in order to make the most significant overall improvement. Occasionally, when I urge students to spend more time practicing their least favorite stroke, they remind me that tennis is supposed to be fun. If forehands are more fun than backhands, why hit backhands? It's a fair question, but I hope the answer is as obvious to you as it is to me. Improving your tennis and winning matches is a lot more fun than playing at a level far below your potential and losing to players you know you can beat.

Work to improve your weakest strokes for the purpose of developing a well-rounded game. If opponents make you hit backhands, respond with effective backhands; if opponents bring you to net, show them effective volleys. A well-rounded game makes you a more offensive player: it is difficult to attack an opponent's weakness when you are busy trying to protect a weakness of your own. A well-rounded player can take advantage of opportunities with forehands as well as backhands, volleys as well as groundstrokes.

For some strokes, you may want more power; for others you may want more control; for still others, you may want to be more consistent. By achieving more balanced and efficient motions, you will be able to reach any or all of these goals. The first step to achieving greater balance and efficiency is knowing when to emphasize hip and shoulder rotation, when to emphasize weight transfer, and when to emphasize a relatively balanced combination of both sources of power.

Index

References to photographs are in italic type.